TRANSFORMING TO A LIFE BEYOND LIMITS
HUPERMAN
BY DUANE WHITE

But we have this treasure in earthen vessels, that the excellence of the power may be of God and not of us.

—2 Corinthians 4:7 (NKJV)

TRANSFORMING TO A LIFE BEYOND LIMITS

HUPERMAN

DUANE WHITE

Beyond These Shores
P.O. Box 1492
Decatur, TX 76234

Unless otherwise indicated, all Scripture quotations are taken from the *King James Version* of the Bible.

Huperman
ISBN 5-919362-93-6
Printed in the United States of America
Copyright ©2006 by Beyond These Shores
P.O. Box 1492
Decatur, TX 76234
(940) 626-4200 phone
(940) 627-0085 fax

Email: info@beyondtheseshores.com
www.beyondtheseshores.com

FORWARD

It always makes me laugh when I hear someone say, "He is an overnight success. He came out of nowhere." The reason I laugh is because life has a way of teaching us the valuable truths we seem to so easily overlook, particularly those that are paramount to fulfilling our destiny. One such principle is that of process. Someone once said, "The real sign of maturity is the ability to put process between the opportunities that present themselves to us and our response to them."

As you read the pages of this book, you will be stirred in your heart to believe the impossible dream. You will awaken to God-possibilities you never knew you possessed and be challenged to rise above the meager levels of just existing. You were born for impact! No one can relate that message any better than my friend, Duane White. The principles you will discover as you read through the pages of this book are not born of theory, but process. He has experienced what he writes. His message is powerful because it flows, not just from the heart of a great student of the Word, but from the passion of a man who has dared to live what he believed.

Let me challenge you as you read to not be casual about what you are learning. There are secrets here that, when embraced as a way of life, will forever break you free from the bounds of mediocrity and allow you to soar into the life you were meant to live. You will discover that you are someone greater than Superman or any other media-produced super hero! You will be excited to know that the real heros of life—the God-filled, Christ-enabled world changers who are impacting every nation of the world— are those unknown ordinary people who are courageous enough to step out of their comfort zones and into the secret place of the Most High God.

That is the invitation being extended to you through the pages of this book. What will your response be? I don't know what your choice will be, but as for me and my house we are being awakened to the Truth that: "I'm not just a husband or a dad. I'm not just a farmer or lawyer. I'm a HUPERMAN!"
Be Blessed!

Bishop Tony Miller
President and Founder of Destiny World Outreach

INTRODUCTION

Several years ago, I was traveling to India to conduct a Pastors' conference when I made a stop in the city of Grimsby in rural England to minister.

As I spoke from 2 Corinthians 4:7: "But we have this treasure in earthen vessels, that the excellency of the power may be of God, and not of us," I explained the Greek prefix *huper*, and talked about how God wants to transform us into a life beyond limits. I also gave my personal testimony. It was a fun evening.

At the conclusion, a very sweet elderly lady came up to me and asked if I had ever heard of the British comedy "Cooperman." I believe it is some kind of spoof. I told her I had not, and she explained a bit about it, and then said, "Well, surely you've heard of Superman—the American superhero."

Of course I had heard of Superman. Everyone has heard of Superman. At this point, I must admit I was wondering where this conversation was headed. The lady went on to explain that while I was preaching, she was getting this revelation of living this outrageously "beyond" life that I was describing. She said, "I kept feeling as though the Lord wanted you to know that you are not Cooperman, nor are you Superman. You are HUPERMAN!"

Something leapt in my spirit.

I was preaching about "Huperman" a few months later in Kenya, and Mike Noviski, a great worship pastor who was traveling with me, heard the message. A few weeks later, I was at Mike's church when he gave me a gift. It was a T-shirt that bore a logo resembling that of Superman with a large "H".

Later, my son suggested I wear the T-shirt whenever I preached on Huperman. That day, Huperman came to life!

I believe everyone has a life's message. No matter where you go or what God does—you seem to come back to one theme. Huperman is just that for me.

For years, people have tried to encourage me to put my teachings into book form. It seemed fitting that my first book should be my life's message. My very bones ache from trying to get people to believe God for something bigger than what they are seeing. I have preached this message all over the world, and have seen amazing breakthroughs as a result.

Just last month, I met a man who heard me preach this in the UK. For nine years he tried to become a fireman. Everyone told him he was too old, and too slow. Then he heard this message.

A few weeks before I met this man, he received not one, but three positions as a fireman. One was a very high position!

When we met, he said to me with a huge smile on his face, "Now that's huper!"

I am afraid to say I don't remember that wonderful lady's name from Grimsby, but on behalf of all those this word has touched, and for all those this book will hopefully inspire—we say, "Thank you!"

ACKNOWLEDGEMENTS

It would be impossible to thank everyone God has used to help bring this book about, but I wanted to thank a few people who really made this happen.

To my darling wife *Kris,* without whom I would not amount to much. You are my best friend! Thanks for putting up with me—not to mention our crazy life and schedule for all these years. You are truly one of the most *huper* people I know!

To the greatest kids on the planet—*Kelsey, Cody* and *Ashton.* Words cannot express how much I love you. You have sown your daddy to the world without complaint, and I know God is going to do *huper* things in each one of you.

Kelsey, I have said it many times but let me say it again—you will always be special to me because you were the first! You made me a daddy and have taught me loads over the years (sometimes I am not sure who is raising whom!). What a beautiful young woman you have become! You're my darlin'.

Cody, my only begotten son. I always dreamed God would give me a son, but I could not have imagined how awesome (and cool) he would be. You are everything I wish I could have been at your age, and God has used you to redeem so many things in my life—not to mention what a good friend you are.

Ashton, you truly are the JOY of our life. You are the *huper* kid God gave us, because you were more than we ever thought of having. That's what's so great about God—His surprises are the best! You are one of the most spiritual people I know, and your relationship with God is incredible. I can't wait to see your orphanage in Africa!

To the awesome team at **BTS.** *Matt,* you are an amazing son in the faith. Thanks for your faithfulness. *Clair,* we can't imagine life without you. You are the best! And thanks for giving us Micah, too. *Candace,* what did we ever do without you? A lot less! You pushed to make this book happen. Thanks! *Alex,* you're the greatest graphic designer in the world! WOW! *Britt and Steph,* you girls light the place up. Thanks for being true servants. Stick around and I will find you husbands (that can also work for us!). *Mama Darlene and Mr. Putchie,* you know what you mean to me and what you mean to this project. But let me say it again–thanks a million.

To my *Mom,* thanks for believing in that little boy that made you cry when you first saw him. You believed for *huper* before I could! And to her awesome husband, *Roy,* thanks for marrying my mom so I don't have to worry about her.

To my *Dad* (and *Malin*), thanks for being my Dad. We missed a lot of years, but God has made up for it. You are a great dad and a great friend. And *Linda,* thanks for putting up with him all these years, keeping him out of trouble and for how you love my kids!

To *Donna,* you are the best sister in the whole world, and one of my best friends! And *Jeff* you have been a real brother not a brother-in-law – we're all glad Donna finally said "yes."

Finally, thanks to *Papa.* If you read in heaven, I want you to know YOU ARE MY HERO!

CHAPTER 1
BREAKING BARRIERS

On May 6, 1954 a British man from Harrow on the Hill named Roger Bannister did something that had never been done. Up until that point experts said it was humanly impossible to run the mile in less than four minutes. They said the human body could not perform such a feat. They called it an unattainable limit—a barrier. But on that day in May 1954, Roger Bannister ran the mile in three minutes, 59.6 seconds. "That's not much less than four minutes," the cynics might argue. And they would be correct. Nonetheless, Bannister broke the barrier. He did what no one else had ever done.

Today, high school athletes routinely run the mile in less than four minutes. But up until that time it was inconceivable. Once Bannister broke that barrier, many people did it.

Matt Berry, one of our team members, told me he was watching a news program in which the commentator remarked that the Olympic record in the 100-meter dash from just a few years ago is now what is used for those qualifying for the Olympics. A pastor friend of mine, Rusty Griffin, says it this way: "Yesterday's excellence is today's mediocrity." The Church—individually and corporately—must come to the realization that not only can God always outdo Himself—He always desires to! He always has something bigger or better up His sleeves. He has big sleeves!

Up until October 14, 1947 no one had ever broken the sound barrier—flown faster than the speed of sound. Test pilot, Chuck Yeager, had tried many times to do it and failed. On October 13, Yeager was horseback riding when the horse decided to go one way while he went the other—landing on the ground and fracturing his ribs.

Yeager had trouble sleeping that night because of the excruciating pain. But that pain did not stop him from getting up the next morning to continue his quest at breaking the sound barrier. He wanted to break this "demon" (as it was referred to at the time), this limit called the sound barrier. No one knew if it was possible. Could a plane when pushed to those limits handle the pressure, or would it blow up? People had all kinds of pre-conceived ideas about what might happen, but Chuck announced he was going to try it. He went on record saying, "I don't know if I can do it or not, but I am going to try. I am going to do my part and then see what happens."

> Barriers are meant to be broken, and once broken, all that's left is breakthrough after breakthrough because we can go beyond the last barrier.

With his rib cage racked with pain, and questions racing through his mind, Yeager climbed into the plane facing all kinds of opposition. *Is this even physically possible?* No one knew.

The plane took off, pressing towards its goal of Mach 1. Yeager's speed climbed to Mach .7. Then, Mach .8 and on towards Mach .9. The closer he got to the "demon," the more violently the plane shook. And the louder became the voices trying to convince him to stop. But Yeager pushed through the opposition—pressing the plane's throttle with a determination to reach the impossible. Suddenly, it happened! BOOM! Chuck Yeager had reached Mach 1! He had broken the sound barrier!

There was no fanfare. Only a few people were watching, because it was a secret mission. And Yeager was forbidden to tell anybody what took place that day. But that didn't change the fact, or the truth that on October 14, 1947, what had been deemed impossible had become reality. Yeager had literally gone where no one had dared go before. Before that day, it had been difficult to even imagine such a time as we live in today—a time of space travel and supersonic speeds. But now it is here. And it all started with that one big BOOM!

Barriers are meant to be broken, and once broken, all that's left is breakthrough after breakthrough because we can go beyond the last barrier. There is always more we can do.

No matter what God does in your life, He always has something else He wants to do. He is an exceeding God. Our problem is that once we have dabbled in a miracle or two, and have seen a blessing here or there, or we receive a break-through, we stop. We sit back and say, "Well, that is wonderful!" and we stop our forward movement. This never should be so, for there are worlds to be explored beyond all the barriers in our lives.

The devil always wants to establish limitations or set up barriers in our lives. These limitations or barriers are known as *"the natural."* By now, you would think he would have learned that all barriers are meant to be broken—that's God's plan. We see people every day who define themselves by their natural limitations. God has given me a heart for those people because I have learned the truth—facts, no matter what they are, do not define a person. I refused to be defined by the facts of my life—and, I refused to be limited by those facts. Instead, I chose to be defined by the truth of God's Word and to be and do and go beyond my natural limitations. For some people, their limiting facts may not be so much physical as emotional. They may define themselves by their experiences. They set up barriers by failures and come to the conclusion they can go no further.

But then we see and hear about people like Roger Bannister, and Chuck Yeager and others like them. They did things the skeptics of their day said were impossible—probably through their own intellect, physical stamina and natural talent. How much more can we do through the supernatural power and wisdom of God?

When people look at the great things God works in the earth through *Beyond These Shores*, they often say, "You know, that is just a normal group of people. They are just an average group of people, but somehow they are doing extremely extraordinary things."

In our own weakness and humanity, God desires for us to believe for uncommon miracles through our common lives, so that when blind eyes open, nobody but God gets the glory. When deaf ears are opened and when the lame begin to walk, only He gets the glory.

CHAPTER 2
THE TRUTH VS THE FACTS

"Ye shall know the truth, and the truth shall make you free" (John 8:32).

In this scripture, Jesus boldly declares that truth has within it the power to transform us from slavery to freedom. Freedom from what? Obviously, the opposite of truth, which is lies. I've learned there's a great difference between the truth and the facts. For many years, the devil used *facts* about my natural circumstances to put limitations on my life. I have walked a lifelong journey trying to understand the difference between the truth and the facts, and have learned a great deal along the way.

The devil will always use facts because the facts are in the natural. We are constantly bombarded with the facts. The media is constantly delivering the facts to us. Whether from the BBC, CNN.com or Newsweek, in this high speed age the facts are readily available. Everywhere you turn, somebody is always ready and willing to tell you *the facts of any particular circumstance.* The biggest problem with this of course is that everyone has their "spins" to the facts to reinforce their own agenda.

> As Christians and people of faith, we don't deny the facts... We just refuse to embrace them.

As Christians and people of faith, we don't deny the facts. We don't bury our heads in the sand and say that something is not real, because we know the facts are evident. We just refuse to embrace them. We understand that the higher reality of God's eternal Truth is greater than the reality of our temporary situations.

While the enemy always deals in the realm of facts, our God always deals in the realm of Truth. Truth exists even when it is not manifested. By that I mean certain things are true in the spirit realm, whether we ever see them manifested in this lifetime or not. I have learned through the years that facts never change the truth; however, God's Truth when applied properly can change the facts.

We see this in 2 Corinthians 10:4-5.

For the weapons of our warfare *are* not carnal, but mighty through God to the pulling down of strong holds; Casting down imaginations, and every high thing that exalteth itself against the knowledge of God, and bringing into captivity every thought to the obedience of Christ.

Here Paul gives us what I believe is a "backwards" progression. He talks about 1) strongholds; 2) vain imaginations; 3) high things; and, 4) thoughts. The enemy always begins with the fourth element— thoughts. He begins by putting a single thought into our mind. That in itself is relatively harmless, but it never remains a single thought.

The thought, if not "captured" immediately, begins to gather friends (other thoughts) that soon begin to go to work in our mind. What are they doing? They are building "high things." The Greek word here is *hupsoma* which literally means a "barrier" or "rampart." The idea is that these thoughts are building a wall or barrier of thought in the mind. The longer they hang around, the higher the wall gets until finally it has "exalted itself" above the knowledge of what God says about the situation (or we could say "the Truth").

Once they are high enough, the enemy begins to connect the walls together and we begin to form images in our mind. Paul calls these images "imaginations." A good friend of mine, Jamie Englehart, refers to them as *image-nations*. Complete nations of thought begin forming "thought patterns."The Greek word here is *logismos*, which means "reasoning that demands a verdict." The images that form through our thoughts now begin to demand a conclusion. The problem is that while this conclusion is congruent with the facts, if its origins are from the enemy, it is always contrary to the Truth.

The result is we end up with a "stronghold" in our mind. The word "stronghold" in the original text is *ochuroma* which literally means a "fortress." At this point we are imprisoned in the castle of our own thought patterns! The enemy will constantly bombard us with a mound of facts that keep piling up in front of us until it is the only image we are able to see. We begin to draw erroneous conclusions from these facts.

What is the answer? Paul says the wall of thoughts is exalted above the "knowledge of God." The only way out of our prison of thinking is by learning to exalt the Truth above the facts! The fact may be that you are sick in your body, but the Truth is that by Jesus' stripes "you are healed" (Isaiah 53:5). The fact may be that your finances are in horrible shape, but the Truth is "my God shall supply all your need according to His riches in glory" (Philippians 4:19). The facts may be that your marriage is struggling and your child is away from God, but the Truth is that "as for me and my house, we will serve the Lord" (Joshua 24:15).

You may say, "Duane, that is simply denial." No, it's not. And I'm not saying you should deny the facts. I'm saying you don't have to embrace them.

In Romans 4 Paul says that Abraham, who the Bible calls the "Father of Faith," *faced the fact* that his body was as good as dead, but he believed God was able to perform what He had promised. When the facts said that Abraham couldn't perform, he believed God could! He exalted the Truth of God's promise above the facts of his present condition.

Paul goes on to say in Romans 4:17 that he understood God "calleth those things that be not as though they were." Many people have gotten this phrase backwards. Paul said God calls things that *are not* as though they *were*, not things that *are* as though they *are not!* Let me repeat that. God calls things that *are not* (yet manifested in the natural) as though they *were* (already manifested), not things that *are* (facts in the natural) as though they *are not* (which is denial)! There is no power in denying the facts. For example, if I say, "I'm not sick, I'm not sick, I'm not sick" over and over, that doesn't change the FACT that I am sick. However, power to change the facts lies in my declaring over and over, "by Jesus stripes I am healed." Why? Because in the latter, I am not denying the facts, I am exalting the Truth! That's what happens when God prophetically declares great things over someone, even though that person is a rascal. He is not denying their flaws, He is speaking things that are not (yet in the natural) as though they were already manifested.

We had the wonderful privilege of living in the beautiful city of Lincoln in rural England for almost two years. Lincoln has one of the greatest cathedrals of England, as well as a magnificent castle. One day while we were touring the castle with friends, the guide began to explain why the turrets are round instead of square. He said originally they were square, but they found that when opposing armies attacked the castle walls, they hit them with huge battering rams, crumbling them and making the fortress penetrable. Eventually, they learned that if they rounded these turrets, the force of the battering ram would actually re-enforce the strength of the defense rather that weaken it.

The Lord began to speak to me immediately about a principle in 2 Corinthians 10. Many people hear a Truth one time, attempt to attack the fortress of thought in their mind and when the wall doesn't immediately fall down, it actually strengthens the argument AGAINST the Truth. Someone gets a revelation about giving, gives one big offering and immediately their finances get worse. Then, they think, *See, that giving stuff doesn't work after all.* Another person hears a truth about healing and prays for a sick friend and they get worse! The conclusion is that healing is not for everyone. We are more intimate with the facts than the Truth.

What is the answer? We must use the spiritual weapons—of prayer, declaring God's Word, praise and worship—to demolish the fortresses in our mind. Like a modern day smart bomb in the unseen realm, we can completely annihilate the enemy's work in our mind. We must learn to stop his thoughts when they first come. Remember that first "thought" we talked about? Paul says to punish it by taking it captive to the obedience of Christ. In other words, we must overcome the facts by exalting the Truth.

For the last several years I have had the privilege of being involved in a great network of churches in the UK called Ground Level, led by Stuart Bell. Annually, they sponsor an event called the Grapevine Celebration, which gathers between 12,000 and 15,000 people each year—many of whom come together and camp for a week while the meetings are held in huge tents.

At one of the celebrations, the weather forecast indicated a downpour of rain would cause us to cancel this annual "Bible Week" (as it's called in the UK). The facts were that it was going to be too muddy, too soggy, and just too messy to have the meeting. The Truth was that God wanted people to come to those meetings.

The event wasn't man's idea, it was God's idea. Every year people are saved, healed, delivered, and receive breakthroughs at these events. We had a choice to make. We could either sit around moaning and groaning about the facts, or we could say, "The time has come for the Truth to change the facts." We declared His will for the event and moved right on with it. The Truth—what God had said to us—prevailed!

We read or hear John 8:32 quoted and think, *If I hear a truth, then that truth will instantly set me free.* However, there are many different words in Greek for the word *know.* In English we use *know* to mean different things. I meet someone one time and I say I know them. If you ask me, "Do you know that person?" I would say yes, but what I mean is I've "met" them. The word "know" in John 8:32 does not mean to simply be introduced to someone or something. It is the Greek word *ginosko.* It means to be "intimately acquainted with," and it is progressive in nature.

I'm set free by the Word of God—the Truth—with which I become intimately acquainted. As I handle the Truth, analyze it, look at it, and embrace it, then I become intimately acquainted with it. It becomes part of me. I become one with it and the Truth begins to make me freer and freer. The enemy's plan is to get us to *ginosko* (be more intimately acquainted with) the facts rather than the Truth. I might have heard a Truth and say "I know that," but the question is, do I *ginosko* it? You see, it is not what we encounter on the journey that predicts our destination, but how we relate to Truth along the way.

CHAPTER 3
ONE BOY'S STORY

My heart's desire is to lead people to the freedom that only Jesus provides, and one of the best ways the Lord has shown me to do that is to simply tell my story. I have shared my story in churches and with individuals around the world. So, in this, my first written message, I'm going to tell my story of how the Truth set me free.

Each one of us has a life message—so individual and unique, no two are alike. We each *are* a message written by the very finger of God.

As you read the story of my journey and how I got where I am today, keep 2 Corinthians 4:7-18 in your mind.

But we have this treasure in earthen vessels, that the excellence of the power may be of God and not of us. *We are* hard-pressed on every side, yet not crushed; *we are* perplexed, but not in despair; persecuted, but not forsaken; struck down, but not destroyed—always carrying about in the body the dying of the Lord Jesus, that the life of Jesus also may be manifested in our body. For we who live are always delivered to death for Jesus' sake, that the life of Jesus also may be manifested in our mortal flesh. So then death is working in us, but life in you. And since we have the same spirit of faith, according to what is written, *"I be-*

lieved and therefore I spoke," we also believe and therefore speak, knowing that He who raised up the Lord Jesus will also raise us up with Jesus, and will present *us* with you. For all things *are* for your sakes, that grace, having spread through the many, may cause thanksgiving to abound to the glory of God. Therefore we do not lose heart. Even though our outward man is perishing, yet the inward *man* is being renewed day by day. For our light affliction, which is but for a moment, is working for us a far more exceeding *and* eternal weight of glory, while we do not look at the things which are seen, but at the things which are not seen. For the things which are seen *are*

> God desires to take very normal, very average, very ordinary people and do extremely extraordinary, extremely supernatural things through them.

temporary, but the things which are not seen *are* eternal *(New King James Version).*

Now here is a man—Apostle Paul—who was shipwrecked, stoned, knocked in the head, bitten by a snake and left for dead. And I get upset when my satellite TV doesn't work. He says this momentary light affliction is working for us a far more exceeding and eternal weight of glory. In verse 7, Paul tells us that we have this treasure in earthen vessels that the excellency (the New International Version says "this all-surpassing power")—of the power might be of God and not of us. The devil is going to constantly tell us the facts about our earthiness. "You are nothing but an earthen vessel—a clay pot." He points out all our flaws, all our mistakes, our hopeless humanity. He constantly rehearses the facts to us. God on the other hand, wants to use that clay pot for His exceeding glory.

I was born on February 27, 1967 with a cleft lip and palate. Today, this birth defect can be routinely repaired through surgical procedures. But in the '60s this wasn't the case. I had a large hole in the roof of my mouth and my lip. No baby pictures were taken of me because they were thought to be "taboo." When my mother saw me, she began to cry because she had never seen a child like this. She said, "How can my son ever speak?"

My mother was a preacher's daughter. She had a dream that her son might preach the Gospel. She looked at me and said, "How can this ever be?"

By the time I was 10 years old I had been in and out of the hospital many times and had multiple surgeries. Although many of these surgeries were performed at such an early age that I don't remember them, there are several that left many painful memories. I remember after one of my surgeries, just before I was released to go home, the doctor came in to remove what seemed to be 50 feet of gauze packed into my nasal cavities. I begged them to put me to sleep, but they said it was unnecessary and it wouldn't hurt much. Apparently, they had never had it done to them, because when they pulled it out I screamed with anguish. It literally felt like my brains were coming out through my nose!

I was poked and jabbed with so many needles I became deathly afraid of the most routine procedures. Once a nurse was simply trying to remove an IV from my arm when (probably as a result of something I did) blood flew all over my face and the bed, resulting in another traumatic experience. I still have the scar on my right side where doctors used a saw to cut out half of one of my ribs and make a hard palate in the roof of my mouth. To this day I cringe at the thought of needles and hospitals.

My nose is a bit flat and as a result, growing up, kids made fun of me. When I moved my family back to Decatur, Texas, where I grew up, it was strange as I drove the streets taking my children to school. I remembered the very playground where kids picked on me. They said, "You will never amount to anything."

I remember looking in the mirror and thinking, *Why am I different? Why am I like this? Why do I have to keep going back to the hospital?* I had to go to the orthodontist because I had teeth growing in the roof of my mouth. Some of them were backwards and they had to put chains on my teeth and mechanisms in my mouth to expand my jaw. These hurt so bad, I thought my head would explode. As a young boy, I remember crying over and over and saying, "I don't understand."

My grandfather was one of my boyhood heroes and my mentor. He was a pastor for 50 years. He drove me 45 miles to the orthodontist to have my teeth worked on every few weeks and sometimes once a week. He drove from Dallas all the way to Decatur, about 60 miles, to pick me up and take me back to Dallas to the orthodontist for my painful appointments.

Back and forth, time after time we traveled together. On the way he told me stories about the goodness of God. I remember one day riding in the car with him and I said, "Pawpaw, why do I have to go through all this?" He said, "Honey, I don't really understand that either, but I believe God has a great plan for your life and will give you the strength to overcome any obstacle."

During these car rides something started rising up in my spirit. I said, "God, I refuse to be defined by these limitations." In my mind I knew the limits were there, but I was born for something greater than what I was experiencing at the moment. I prayed, "I don't look right and people make fun of me, but if You will just anoint me, if You will just empower me, if You will just help me—then I will go anywhere You tell me to go. I will do anything You tell me to do. I'll say anything You tell me to say." The reality of the Truth of the Word of God began to rise in my heart.

Other things happened to me as a child. When I was 12 years old, my dad left my mom and they went through a bitter divorce. (Today my dad and I have a great relationship, so he doesn't mind my telling this story.) I went through a struggle, thinking, *I don't have a dad. How am I ever going to amount to anything?* As a teenager I remember sitting on the living room floor with a gun in my hand—the thought running through my mind: *If you kill yourself, you can leave a note and beg your parents to get back together. That would be the greatest thing you could do with your life.* The enemy was trying to build an *image-nation* that would destroy my life and destiny, as well as deeply wound those I loved. This was simply a lie that was trying to exalt itself above the Truth.

Throughout my younger days, the devil kept telling me, "You are just a clay pot that can never do anything." He was absolutely right—that was a fact. But having learned the Truth very early on, I always kept in mind what Paul told the Corinthians—that we have a treasure in jars of clay (2 Corinthians 4:7). I began to understand that the treasure is the resurrection life of Jesus. He says this treasure has been invested in very average, very ordinary people. That says to me that the more normal, the more average, the more ordinary someone realizes he is, the greater glory God receives.

The Greek word in 2 Corinthians 4:7 for "excellency" is the word *huperbole*. We would say "hyperbole." Hyperbole is an extravagant exaggeration. Teenagers are great at hyperbole. Everything is extreme. Everything is the "-est". Almost everything is an exaggeration. My oldest daughter is now a teenager, and it is amazing to me how she has learned (along with her friends) to perfect the use of hyperbole. If a room is a little warm, "it's the hottest room in the world!" If it is a little chilly, "it is the coldest place on earth." God wants to make our lives one huge hyperbole!

According to Paul, God desires to take very normal, very average, very ordinary people and do extremely extraordinary, extremely supernatural things through them. When other people look at them, they say, "Wow! That can't be that person. That must be God."

A few years back, I was honored to make the

acquaintance of a ministry called Betel International, led by Elliot and Mary Tepper and based in Madrid, Spain. This great organization is a community primarily made up of ex-drug addicts and individuals who have been completely marginalized by society. These men and women, many of whom are literally rescued from living on the streets, are not only set free from drug and alcohol abuse, but are then molded into pastors

exceedingly + abundantly + beyond (above)

"huper" (super, hyper)

"perissos" (to go beyond a particular measure or boundary) ↳ the very best you can be

"huper"

Adding "huper" to any word, phrase, or idea, takes it to its fullest extent and then beyond whatever limit or measure that may be set or expected. HUPER takes anything "beyond" itself.

and leaders who are ultimately sent to plant churches around the world. You would think somebody forgot to tell these people that drug addicts can't plant churches! The people they send out—not just earthen vessels, but once-broken, now-restored vessels—do everything by the excellency of God. They have no limits and no barriers because God has no limits!

CHAPTER 4
YOU CAN'T KILL A DEAD MAN

We Christians know we have this treasure in us that Paul speaks about. We know the resurrection life of Jesus is in us. Paul tells us the power lies within us to keep going beyond our limits. We are troubled on every side, but we are not distressed. We are perplexed, but we are not in despair. We are persecuted, but we are not forsaken. We are struck down, but we are not destroyed.

In times past I read that and thought, *Oh, this is so terrible.* Today I see Paul's words in a different light. He says in verse 10 that we are always bearing about in our bodies the dying of the Lord Jesus that the life of Jesus might be made manifest in our body.

To get the treasure out of the jar, the treasure has to be exposed. One of the ways to get to the treasure is to break the jar. Now, I come from a particular theological stance that says God doesn't go around breaking jars. Some people disagree with that stance, and that's fine—we all have our opinion. I don't believe God gives people things like cancer to prove a point. I don't believe God abuses His children to teach them lessons.

I believe if a jar gets broken, the devil is the one who breaks it. He tries to push you far enough into a corner so that you are beat down. His goal is to define you, to limit you, and finally to defeat you. So he piles up the trouble in your life to try to destroy you.

Paul's understanding knocks the devil right in the head. He said, "I have been crucified with Christ; it is no longer I who live, but Christ lives in me; and the *life* which I now live in the flesh I live by faith in the Son of God, who loved me and gave Himself for me" (Galatians 2:20, NKJV).

> If I can "reckon" God's grace properly in my life, I can access all God has deposited in my spiritual account "in Christ."

So what is Paul saying? He is saying that when Jesus died, I died. I am no longer in Adam, but I am in Christ.

I often use an illustration to make the point more clear. Suppose I take one of my youngest daughter's dolls and put it in a large cereal box. I close the lid and begin to do crazy things to the box. I jump on it. I throw it in the air. Tell me, what happens to the doll? She is dropped from several feet in the air to the ground. She is beaten and crushed. Why? Because she is in the box. Whatever happens to the box happens to the doll! It's the law of heredity. The author of Hebrews said that Levi paid tithes to Melchizedek. In other words, Levi got credit for paying tithes to Melchizedek when Abraham paid tithes to Melchizedek. How is that possible, when Levi was Abraham's great grandson? He was not even alive when this event took place. Because, Hebrews says, he was in Abraham's loins. Before I was born, I was in my mother's womb. Before I was in my mother's womb, I was in my daddy's loins (to use King James verbage) and before I was in my daddy's loins, I was in my granddaddy's loins, and so on. All the way back to Adam. I was born "in Adam." So everything that happened to Adam (mankind) happened to me. Some people think I'm a pretty good person. I've never killed anyone. I've never committed adultery. I've never done this or that.

That may be a fact, but according to the law of

heredity that is not Truth. Since you are born "in Adam," then just like Levi, the decisions of your ancestors are credited to your spiritual account. Everything they did—you did. But the good news is that 2 Corinthians 5:17 says if any man be "in Christ" he is a new creature. So everything that happened to Christ happened to me. When He died, I died spiritually.

Paul understood that all of this trouble that the devil meant to destroy me with is *momentary light affliction.* When I am snakebitten, all it does is remind me I am "dead". When I am persecuted, I remember I am "dead". When somebody offends me, I am "dead".

What does a dead man do? A dead man just lays there. So Apostle Paul says, "Devil, you cannot break my jar because my jar was broken when Christ's passion broke Him. If you saw the movie, *The Passion of the Christ* you saw every-thing Jesus went through. And because we are in Him, it happened to us. We died with Him. However, if I died with Him, then I must also be raised with Him! Why? Because if I am in Christ, then everything that happened to Him happened to me. Over and over in the New Testament we see the phrases, "in Him," "in Christ," "in the Lord," "in the Spirit," and "in Whom." Well, that's you and me. If you are in Christ you can put your name in those verses.

Throughout his letter to the Romans, Paul talked about *reckoning.* The word *reckon* in the Greek is an accounting term. It means to "balance the books" like a system of credits and debits. We must reconcile some things in our thinking. What happens if you don't reconcile your bank statement properly? Your checks will bounce, or maybe you will have money you didn't know you had. If I can reckon God's grace properly in my life, I can access all God has deposited in my spiritual account "in Christ."

In Romans 6:11, (New King James Version), he said, "Reckon yourselves to be dead indeed to sin, but alive to God in Christ Jesus our Lord." I believe Paul lived as a dead man. A dead man can't be offended. Whenever he was tempted by the devil to be offended, he would say, "I reckon I'm dead." When the devil tempts us to be offended we must do the same thing Paul did. *They hurt my feelings.* Your feelings can't be hurt if you're dead. *They didn't let me prophesy last Sunday.* Dead people can't get angry because no one let them prophesy. *I got laid off my job and people were mean to me.* That can't bother you because you are dead.

Paul told the church at Colossae, "For you died, and your life is hidden with Christ in God" (Colossians 3:3, NKJV). Your life is hid. You're hidden, and you cannot be found. Most Christians have near-death experiences. They almost die, and then they say, "Oh, excuse me, what about this or that point?" Your dead man doesn't have a "point." "But, but—excuse me." No, your dead man doesn't have a "but."

The challenge here is that we build our theology on the idea that we have two natures. We say, "I am fighting my old man. My old man tried to rise up." How can a dead man rise up? If he is dead, he is dead. Paul said my old man was crucified with Christ.

Then Paul asks himself these questions, according to Romans 7:15-20: "Why do I do the things that I don't want to do? And I don't do the things I want to do? And the things I want to do, I don't do; and the things I don't want to do, I do?"

You might think he was confused about it all.

Sometimes we all feel just like Paul. The truth is, we are not fighting the old man. We are fighting the memory of who we once were, and memories are powerful!

My grandfather, who helped build my faith in the Truth of God's Word, passed away a few years ago, but his memory is still very much alive in me. When I hear the old hymn *Just as I Am,* my thoughts go immediately to my grandfather. It was his favorite song. When I think of him, he becomes so real. I can even smell him. He is right there with me. Why? Because memories are powerful. They can make us feel something right

now that was in the past. This is why Jesus said
of Communion, "Do this in remembrance of me."
The word *remember* is to "relive the experience all
over again." When we remember the Cross we
are reckoning it so in our lives.

What's left of our old man is simply our memories. And the more I can reckon what happened
supernaturally when I became a new man in
Christ, the more it manifests naturally. Paul had
experienced enough tests that he knew that the
very thing the devil tried to use to destroy him,
God used to deliver him. The same is true for
you and me. The very trouble that tries to kill me
is going to prove that I am already "dead", and
you cannot kill a dead man.

CHAPTER 5

TREASURE EXPOSED

Back to our jar of clay—how *do* we get this treasure out of the jar? We do it by reckoning that our jar was broken in Christ. Once we do that, nothing the devil does can hurt us. All his efforts actually work to produce in us the eternal weight of God's glory Paul told us about.

The Lord gave me a message about the difference between consumers and producers. All of us fall into one of those two categories. Without attempting to preach that entire message here, let me simply explain its application for our purposes.

We can either be consumed by our pain, or we can use our pain to produce the glory of God—His Anointing in our life. Two people can go through the same or similar experiences. One will come out with a testimony. The other will come out with a tragedy. What makes the difference? Really, there is no difference. They both get what they reckoned their experience would be. If I reckon my situation to be an opportunity to see God's glory, that is what it will be. If I reckon it is something to destroy me, then that is what it will be. The better we un-

> We can either be consumed by our pain, or we can use our pain to produce the glory of God— His Anointing in our life.

derstand that we were broken 2000 years ago in Christ, the more we can identify with His death and His Resurrection.

The same Spirit that raised Christ from the dead will quicken our mortal body (Romans 8:11). Paul's perspective was, "Go ahead and hit me with your best shot because all it will do is produce the resurrection life of Jesus in me." Remember the "Rocky" movie where Sylvester Stallone is fighting Mr. T? There comes a point where Mr. T's character (I think he was called Clubber Lang) begins to pound on Rocky. Suddenly Rocky puts his boxing glove up to his chin as if to say, "Come on hit me again!" He keeps taunting his aggressor saying, "It ain't so bad!" We need to become like Rocky and reckon that the enemy's worst blow only helps release the life of God in us.

In 2 Corinthians 4:12 (NKJV), he said, "Death is working in us, but life in you." In other words, "What is killing me—the worst thing I might go through—is delivering you, Corinthians."

As for me, the devil thought, *I will give this boy a cleft lip and palate. I will slap him around a little bit. I will abuse him. I'll have his parents break up.*

I will have kids make fun of him. All the time he thought he was digging me a grave—putting stuff on me that would kill my spirit. The grave was there for me to fall into and the mound of dirt was piling up. But when I realized I had already died with Christ, the grave that was meant to hold me down and the soil that was meant to cover me up became the very platform I climbed up on to proclaim God's goodness.

See, the very dirt that the devil digs out of the ground to destroy you with—no matter what form it takes—will be the very platform God uses to get people saved, healed, and delivered as you give Him glory. I find it totally amazing—totally God—that the dirt the devil uses on us simply becomes the place for God's Anointing to bring Him glory.

I mentioned earlier that our family lived in England for almost two years. Originally, we were only planning to stay in the UK for six months to establish a sort of missions beachhead from which we could launch into Europe more effectively. We were working primarily with Stuart Bell, the apostolic overseer of the Ground Level network of churches and Senior Pastor of New Life Christian Fellowship in Lincoln, England. While we were in that initial six-month period, Stuart's 16-year-old son, David, noticed his eye swelling, and it never seemed to go down. David was a very healthy and athletic young man, so we just thought it might have been an infection of some kind. After seeing a doctor, David was told to go for testing and ultimately a biopsy was ordered. I was at the hospital when the doctor gave them the prognosis from his biopsy. David had a very rare form of eye cancer.

We immediately began to speak the Word of the Lord over David and began fighting to see the manifestation of God's healing in his eye. Today, I am happy to say that David is completely healed and cancer free! To really do this story justice would take too long for this short message. The point is that the enemy had a plan to destroy a great young man's life, but God used that circumstance to bring healing not only to David, but to all those he will reach in his lifetime. He now is anointed to heal the sick. His boldness overwhelms me. Even in the hospital, he was praying for healing for all those kids in the cancer ward. He has a great disdain for that horrible disease and is always eager and ready to pray for those whom the devil is trying to destroy with it. The

very soil the enemy tried to bury David with is
now his platform to reach others.

CHAPTER 6
CHOOSE YOUR WEAPONS

Instead of having a near-death experience, you just ought to go ahead and take hold of your death in Christ with all you've got. You have to believe it. Paul says what sounds like some crazy things in 2 Corinthians 4:13. He said we, like David, have received a spirit of faith. Then, he goes on to explain that because of this spirit of faith, we believe and therefore we speak. Faith people speak some pretty crazy things. A minister was asked, "Are you one of those faith preachers?" His immediate response was, "What other kind is there?" Those who preach doubt and unbelief.

If you are preaching the Good News, it must be by faith. Everything we do is by faith. I understand that many people have abused the principles of faith, but we can't simply abandon a scriptural principle because of them. Paul said that we speak what we believe.

When David was only a young shepherd, he understood this principle. He came out to battle Goliath and said, "Hey there, you uncircumcised Philistine. Who do you think you are to come against my God?"

Here's this boy, a teenager, who's been taking care of a few sheep on the back side of the desert. He went to the battlefield, carrying a little lunch to his brothers. He saw what was going on and wanted to know, "Who is that guy?" They told him that this was the champion of the Philistines.

David marched right up to Goliath and said, "You are not much of a champion. Who do you think you are?"

He told the giant, "Today I am going to cut off your head, and I am going to feed it to the birds." Now that is a bold statement from a boy who doesn't even have a pocket knife. He knew he didn't have the weapon to cut off that huge head. How was he going to do it then? With Goliath's sword. What was Goliath's sword created to do? Kill his enemy. Who was David? Goliath's enemy. So you see, the very weapon which was created and designed to destroy David became the weapon God used to cut off the head of the Israelites' enemy.

> The very weapon which was created and designed to destroy David became the weapon God used to cut off the head of the Israelites' enemy.

Has it ever occurred to you that the very thing that has tormented you—the thing you have been afraid of—might be the very thing God will use to deliver you—if you stand up and start speaking to it?

David did not tell God how big Goliath was. He told Goliath how big God was!

Jesus said in Mark 11:23, "For verily I say unto you, That whosoever shall say unto this mountain, Be thou removed, and be thou cast into the sea; and shall not doubt in his heart, but shall believe that those things which he saith shall come to pass; he shall have whatsoever he saith." As a young boy, I heard that scripture preached and wondered why, when I spoke to my "mountains" they didn't seem to go away instantly. One day I was studying this verse and discovered something that changed my thinking. The word "doubt" in the Greek is the word *diakrine,* which means "to judge, criticize, or to separate yourself from what you said." So what Jesus is saying is this: "If you will speak God's Word to your problems, and not give up on your confession, eventually you will have what you say." It's not that you just speak to something one time, and like a magic wand—presto—it is done! Rather, when God gives you a Word about a situation, you have to get into agreement with what He says about that thing and keep holding on to your profession of faith (Hebrews 4:14), until it manifests in the natural.

But here is what we often do. We face a mountain in life, and we run to our prayer closet and say, "Oh, God, do you see how big my mountain is? My mountain is bigger than anyone else's mountain. Oh, God, would you please think about maybe taking this mountain down a little at a time?"

I remember facing so many mountains in my life when I was a teenage boy. A preacher once made a statement that I never forgot (and have repeated many times!). There comes a time in our life where we need to quit whining and moaning and bellyaching to God about how big our mountain is, and turn to our mountain and declare how big our God is! Hebrews 13:5-6 says that the Lord will never leave us or forsake us, so we may BOLDLY say that He is our helper and we will not fear what man will do to us. God said things about us so that we may BOLDLY say some things as well! What is God saying about your situation? He is saying it so you may BOLDLY declare it as well.

Hebrews also says God framed the world with His words. Do you realize you are made in God's image and likeness, and you frame your world with your words? When you say what God says about your world, you are framing the borders of your tomorrow. Your life today is a picture of your words yesterday. And your world tomorrow is being framed by your words today!

CHAPTER 7
BREAKING THROUGH

Remember that Grapevine conference I wrote about earlier? Well, when it looked as though we would be rained out, Stuart came to me and said, "Let's take a little *prophetic* drive." I said, "Yes, sir. Let's go." So, in the pouring rain, we drove down the back roads of rural Lincolnshire that border the showgrounds where Grapevine is held. Stuart said, "We have half an hour to move these clouds or the event will have to be canceled." I said, "Yes, sir."

We began to speak to the clouds, saying, "You cannot come beyond this point in the road." It started raining more. Stuart looked at me, and I looked at him, and we started praying in tongues. We spoke to the rain, "Rain, you cannot come on this side of this road." We just kept speaking our faith.

After a while we made our way back to the conference grounds. As we drove up, the rain stopped. The people who were working there said, "It is a miracle!" We decided our plan had worked pretty well and were feeling pretty good about ourselves. So we decided to drive around

> We kept speaking to that "mountain" until it moved.

the conference grounds seven times—one time for every day we needed dry weather.

As we began our drive, some of our team

joined us. A journalist wanting to interview Stuart about the event was there, and we said, "We are doing serious kingdom business here. You can have your interview while we drive. Get in!" So he rode around with us.

We made seven laps and not a drop of rain fell. We stopped the car and were feeling pretty good again. We sat down and the rain started again. Stuart looked at me, and I looked at him, and we had a choice to make. We could either retreat and give in to these facts, or we could say, "No, we are not going to be denied. It may be raining but we are going to keep speaking to these clouds until they move." We got in the car and continued to drive around the grounds.

Now, I'm sure we weren't the only ones praying—thousands of faithful, eager-to-meet-with-God people were registered for this conference. But we knew we had a job to do, so we simply did our part. It was amazing to see what God did. The rain subsided and the event rolled on. Years later I am still receiving testimonies of what God did in those meetings.

God taught us something that day. We were tempted to go and beg God to move those clouds, as if He didn't really want to do it and our praying would somehow coerce Him to change His mind. No, we simply had to speak the Truth over that situation until we saw a breakthrough. We kept speaking to that "mountain" until it moved.

CHAPTER 8
BEYOND YOU

I have two scriptures that I call my "life scriptures": Ephesians 3:20 and 1 Corinthians 2:9.

Ephesians 3:20 says, "Now unto him that is able to do exceeding abundantly above all that we ask or think, according to the power that worketh in us."

The New American Standard version says,

"...who is able to do far more abundantly beyond all that we ask..."

I like that word "beyond." Beyond what? Beyond me. Beyond my abilities and natural limitations. God loves to go beyond all that I could ever dream of.

The three Greek words there for exceedingly, abundantly and beyond (or above) gave me a picture of myself that has changed my life. First, let's look at "abundantly." The Greek word is *perissos*. This word means "to go beyond a particular measure or boundary." It means "full in stature, pre-eminent, supreme." So, in your life it would mean "the very best you can be in every area of your life." That's the nature of God in us—to make us the best we could ever dream of being.

For some that would be a major improvement—to just be the best they could be with their God-given talents and intellect. However, that is not what Paul was saying here. He wasn't saying, "YOU do your best to improve yourself and that will be good enough. You be all you can be and God will be happy." No, he doesn't leave the word *perissos* alone, but takes it a step further. He didn't say God is able to do just "abundantly." He says God does EXCEEDING abundantly. And the word "exceeding" is the prefix I told you about earlier, used in the word *huperbole.* It is the Greek word *huper.* It sounds like "super" but with an *h,* and in English it is our word "hyper."

Adding *huper* to any word, phrase or idea, takes it to its fullest extent and then beyond whatever limit or measure that may be set or expected. *Huper* takes any thing beyond itself.

Huper would be like you playing in a soccer match (football to my British friends) which you are winning 5-0 with only a few seconds remaining in the match, and you score five more goals. The idea is so far out, it is almost ridiculous.

Paul is stressing his point here. He says God has put the power to work in each of us, to be and do the very best we can be and do, AND, He is going to do some more on top of that. He has provided "*huper* anointing." It is like the motto of Buzz Lightyear from the movie *Toy Story*—"To infinity and BEYOND!"

It is important to notice the source of our power on the journey to "beyond." He says here it is according to the power that is at work in us. That is interesting to me. He didn't say that it is according to the power that is in us, but the power that is *at work* in us. Therefore, we can have the Resurrection power of God in us, but that

> God loves to go beyond all that I could ever dream of.

doesn't necessarily mean it is *at work* in us. How do we get this power to go to work? Remember the text in 1 Corinthians? These momentary light afflictions are producing in us a far more *huper* release of the glory of God. Trials, when reckoned properly, release the *huper* Resurrection power of God in our life. The power of God is activated and put to work in us when trials come. A *huper* Anointing is released when we reckon that we died in Christ and are raised with Him. His *huper* power in us takes us beyond the situations that might otherwise destroy us and releases the treasure that has been hidden in our earthen vessel.

It is also important to realize that He says it is according to the power at work in YOU. God doesn't do things beyond you according to the power that is working in someone else, but according to the power that is working in you. That is why someone else's testimony can encourage you, but it cannot produce this kind of *huper* release in your life. Only your testimony can do that.

CHAPTER 9
HUPERMAN IS ALIVE AND WELL
- IN YOU!

In the Old Testament the Anointing came "upon" men or women. They received the Anointing for tasks at hand. For example, the Anointing came upon Elijah and he ran faster than the chariots of Ahab to Jezreel. The Bible tells us that he girded up his loins—that means he pulled up his trousers—and he ran. How did he do that? He did it by the Anointing that came upon him.

In the New Testament the Anointing comes "out of" us. We have an Anointing, an unction from the Holy One, and it is inside. God is able to take our very best efforts and resources and do some more on top of that. That's a great deal!

In Ephesians 3, Paul doesn't stop with just one *huper*. What he actually says is, "Now unto him who is able to do *huper perissos huper.*" *Perissos* (the best of my abilities) is sandwiched between two slices of *huper*. The Greek word for "beyond" or "above all" is also the word *huper*.

God is able to take the very, very, very best YOU and do even more than that. Then He is able to do more on top of that! Paul says, God is able to do *huper*, or beyond, whatever you could ask or think. The idea of to "ask or think" is "your wildest thoughts, dreams, or imagination. Just close your eyes for five seconds. Think about the wildest, craziest, most insane thing that God could do in your life. Now open your eyes and read on—God is bigger than that!

What is your wildest dream? Is it to have a great ministry? Start a kingdom business? Have a successful marriage and family? God wants to do more than that!

As a young man, I had many dreams and aspirations of traveling the world and preaching the Gospel. I can honestly say that He has already exceeded most of them (and I am still a young man). I dreamed that God would give me a wonderful wife and children. How could this be with a hair-lipped boy who could hardly get a date? And would my children be scarred for life like me? How could I cope with that? God had a *huper* plan. There is no way in this little book I could tell just how my *huper* manifested, but let me tell you – it did!

In 1991 God let me marry the most wonderful woman in the world. She was tailor-made for me. Everything I asked God for in a wife, He gave to me, and many things I wasn't even smart enough to ask for. She is my best friend and has been used by God to prove His never ending love for me. She is a great mother and an amazing partner in ministry. BEYOND all that, she is incredibly good-looking! As a teenage boy, I never dreamed I could have landed such a beauty, but God had *huper* plans.

Then He gave me the three greatest children in the world – Kelsey, Cody, and Ashton. We have two gorgeous daughters (who take after their mother) and a wonderful son in the middle. They are amazing! Somehow they cope with our crazy ministry schedule and love God with all their hearts. I am so proud to be their father. In all my wildest dreams I never believed God would do something so wonderful for me. He is a *huper* God!

God wants to do exceedingly abundantly above and beyond *your* wildest dreams. If He did it for me, He will do it for you. He has *huper* Anointing for you. He wants to take you beyond what is normal and reasonable and acceptable.

He wants to take your life and make it so extravagant with His presence that only He can get the credit.

God is an exceeding, abundantly-above God. Read your Bible. See Him in action from Genesis to Revelation and right on through to today. And you will see that He takes ordinary, normal people and things and uses them in exceeding, abundantly-above ways.

See God in action providing for the salvation of mankind. The death of the lamb has always provided salvation, and with each lamb, each deliverance was exceeding, abundantly-above the former deliverance. My friend, partner, and spiritual mentor, Bishop Tony Miller, says it this way: "One lamb was offered for one man—for Isaac on the mount. Then one lamb was slain for a household—the children of Israel in Egypt. Then a lamb was offered for a whole nation—Israel, each year on the day of atonement. Finally, one lamb was crucified for all of mankind—Jesus on the cross."

You may say, "Well, there you go, God can't exceed that!" However, think about this, more people are alive on the planet today than the cumulative history of mankind. So the blood of Jesus is doing more to redeem mankind that it has ever done in history. And tomorrow it will do even more, and the next day it will do more, and so on and so on.

God is an exceeding, abundantly-beyond God. This is my life's message. All my passion is wrapped up in it. I want to infuse it into everyone who hears it.

No doubt, you have heard of the American comic book hero, Superman. Back in the 1950s, his adventures were put on television and since then he has been portrayed in several major motion pictures.

Clark Kent—Superman's alter ego—was what my generation would call a "dork." He was a mild-mannered news reporter. He wasn't even a good news reporter because he was never present when the news story was breaking. I would have fired him.

There were stark differences between Clark and Superman. Clark wore ugly glasses—Superman had X-ray vision. Clark dressed very plain. Superman—well, you know. Clark loved Lois Lane. He was always trying to get Lois to like him. But he was way too average, too ordinary for Lois. She liked Superman—who always, somehow showed up when trouble arose. Now, when trouble came, Clark seemed to disappear. Little did anyone know that he was hunting a phone booth.

> I know I am just a little boy born with a cleft lip and palate who found a phone booth.

He came out of that phone booth, but, instead of running away from trouble, he headed straight for it. He was asking, "Where is my phone booth? Give me just a minute. I'm going to change into another man—the real me—and when I get back, I am going to face my trouble. I can change because I understand that I am not from this planet,

I am from Krypton. And you cannot touch me."
He was faster than a speeding bullet…more
powerful than a locomotive…able to leap tall
buildings in a single bound. Is it a bird? No. Is
it a plane? No, it's Superman. You know the story.

I go all over the world, not as an American, but
as a representative of the Kingdom of God. You
may see yourself as a mild-mannered, average
Clark Kent-type. You may feel like your life is
filled with ordinary things. I want you to understand you do not have to find an external phone
booth—everything you need is within you. You
have the Anointing of Almighty God. The Holy
One—the Anointed One and His Anointing—
Jesus, lives in you. Make 1 John 4:4 your theme:
"Greater is He that is in me than he that is in the
world."

It is a privilege for me to travel to the nations of the world, but sometimes I ache for the
masses—not because of their poverty or living
conditions per say, but rather because of another deficiency in their lives—they are simply

too reserved about God. I see them in sporting arenas and they aren't reserved there. When it's time for the FIFA World Cup, the nations know how to celebrate. People line the streets, fly their national flag out the window and throw extravagant parties. These same people relinquish their enthusiasm for dead religion when it comes to God and Church.

I believe the Church needs to get a spirit of excitement and celebration to help the world understand how exciting life in the Kingdom of God really is. We need to loosen up. We need to let the world know that we are not of this planet.

We are not of Texas. We are not of America or Great Britain. We are citizens of Heaven. We are children of the living God.

We have to be determined and boldly say, "I will not be limited by the things I see in me or around me. I will throw away those old ways of seeing things (get rid of Clark's glasses). I will discard those old ways of doing things. I will loosen my tie. I will take off my shirt." Paul said,

"I will put off my old man, and I will put on the new man" (Colossians 3:9-10). I will not worry about what anyone thinks of me. I lay down my dignity when it comes to being God's new man.

You have to make up your mind to let that treasure in you be exposed.

The world is waiting for your miracle. I know that is true, because it is true in my life. The devil said, "I'll define him by giving him a cleft lip." Little did he know that he provided the very thing that God would use to bring deliverance—not just to me, but to nations around the world. God uses me as a prophetic trumpet to nations. The devil tried to stop me, but God did exceeding, abundantly beyond anything I could ever dream. And my dreams are still coming and keep getting larger because my treasure is still pouring out.

I am not the greatest orator you will ever hear. I am not the most intellectual or the most gifted or the most talented preacher you will ever meet. But I may be the most thankful.

I am not supposed to be able to speak. I am not supposed to be able to stand and proclaim God's goodness, but that's why I never think for one minute that the purpose of my life has anything to do with me. I know I am just a little boy born with a cleft lip and palate who found a phone booth.

You, like Clark Kent, may start out in life as a mild-mannered, average, ordinary person. The circumstances of your life may be trying to mold you into mediocrity, but today if you can reckon who you are in Christ, you can step into your phone booth and be changed into another person.

Then the monologue of your life will be: *"They are faster than any fiery darts of the wicked one...more powerful than any forces of darkness...able to run through a troop and leap over a wall in a single bound."*

Is it a bird? No!

Is it a plane? No!

Who is it?

It's HUPERMAN!

About the Author

God's purposes always prevail! Born with a cleft lip and palate, Duane White's parents were told he could never speak without impediment. However, God had a purpose. Through faith and patience, Duane developed his speaking ability and followed after his boyhood heroes—preachers of the Gospel! Duane's grandfather, (a 60-year veteran of ministry) who pioneered many churches, was a special inspiration to him. With his special insight into the value of speech, Duane dedicated his mouth and voice to God. He preached his first sermon at 13 years old and hasn't stopped since! He knows his mouth was given to him to fulfill his destiny!

After graduation from high school, Duane spent a few years as a horse-trader and auctioneer. In early 1987, however, he left the horse business to pursue the call on his life by attending Christ For The Nations Institute in Dallas, TX. While attending CFNI, he was involved in pioneering Family Christian Center in Azle, Texas, where he served full-time as part of the leadership team for more than 11 years.

In 2000, Duane, his wife, Kris, and their three children, Kelsey, Cody, and Ashton, launched Beyond These Shores, a missions network that connects ordinary people to their extra-ordinary destiny! Their vision is to equip, empower and engage the local church worldwide to go beyond the limits of past experiences into God's abundance.

Duane travels the world stirring passion in God's people and equipping Church leaders. Over the past 10 years, he has trained tens of thousands of leaders around the globe. He has a BA degree from Advantage College and a Master of Ministry in Leadership from Southwestern Christian University. He serves on the leadership teams of various churches and networks in the UK and the United States. Duane uses his dynamic preaching style with a strong emphasis on the prophetic, to release destiny in the nations of the earth. He is sure to challenge you to get a vision for something "bigger than yourself" as you engage with your calling and discover the purposes God has for your life. His very life testifies that no obstacle is large enough to stand in the way of your destiny!